초등 영어독해를 쉽고 재미있게!

똑똑한 초등영어독해 Starter 1 [개정판]

초등 영어독해를 쉽고 재미있게!
똑똑한 초등영어독해 Starter 1 [개정판]

2007년 11월 06일 초판 1쇄 펴냄
2022년 10월 25일 개정 1쇄 펴냄

지은이 국제어학연구소 영어학부
감수 Jenny Kim
그림 유지환

펴낸이 이규인
펴낸곳 국제어학연구소 출판부

출판등록 2010년 1월 18일 제302-2010-000006호
주소 서울특별시 마포구 대흥로4길 49, 1층(용강동 월명빌딩)
Tel (02) 704-0900 **팩시밀리** (02) 703-5117
홈페이지 www.bookcamp.co.kr
e-mail changbook1@hanmail.net
ISBN 979-11-9792031-8 13740
정가 13,000원

영어의 기초를 다져 주는
magic 시리즈

초등 영어 독해를 쉽고 재미있게!

똑똑한

Starter ❶
[개정판]

초등 영어독해

글 국제어학연구소 영어학부 | 감수 Jenny Kim | 그림 유지환

국제어학연구소

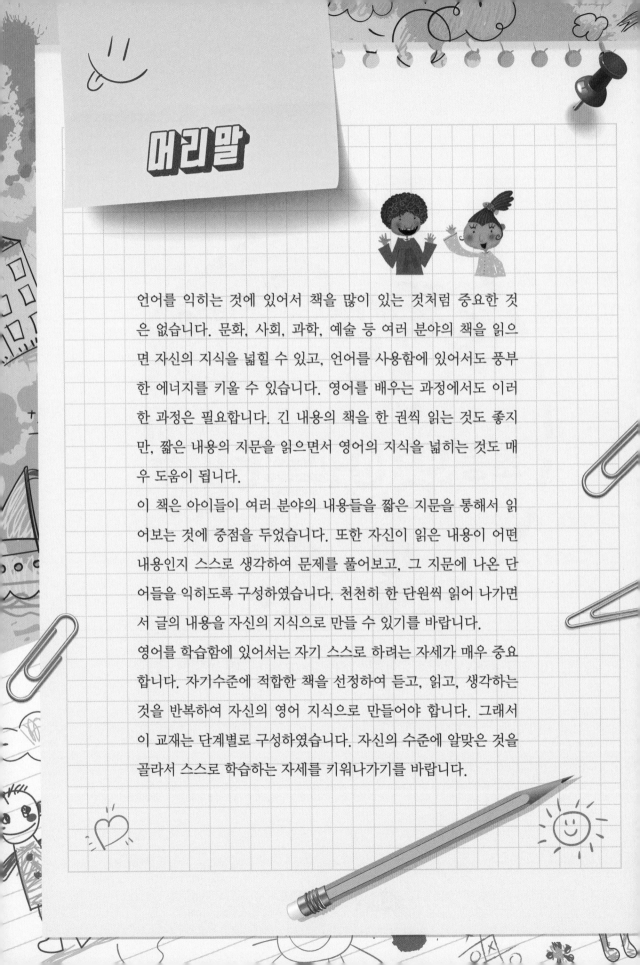

머리말

언어를 익히는 것에 있어서 책을 많이 있는 것처럼 중요한 것은 없습니다. 문화, 사회, 과학, 예술 등 여러 분야의 책을 읽으면 자신의 지식을 넓힐 수 있고, 언어를 사용함에 있어서도 풍부한 에너지를 키울 수 있습니다. 영어를 배우는 과정에서도 이러한 과정은 필요합니다. 긴 내용의 책을 한 권씩 읽는 것도 좋지만, 짧은 내용의 지문을 읽으면서 영어의 지식을 넓히는 것도 매우 도움이 됩니다.

이 책은 아이들이 여러 분야의 내용들을 짧은 지문을 통해서 읽어보는 것에 중점을 두었습니다. 또한 자신이 읽은 내용이 어떤 내용인지 스스로 생각하여 문제를 풀어보고, 그 지문에 나온 단어들을 익히도록 구성하였습니다. 천천히 한 단원씩 읽어 나가면서 글의 내용을 자신의 지식으로 만들 수 있기를 바랍니다.

영어를 학습함에 있어서는 자기 스스로 하려는 자세가 매우 중요합니다. 자기수준에 적합한 책을 선정하여 듣고, 읽고, 생각하는 것을 반복하여 자신의 영어 지식으로 만들어야 합니다. 그래서 이 교재는 단계별로 구성하였습니다. 자신의 수준에 알맞은 것을 골라서 스스로 학습하는 자세를 키워나가기를 바랍니다.

이 책의 구성

Before Reading

스토리에 대한 이해도를 높이기 위하여 새로운 단어와 중요 표현을 미리 익혀요.

Story

앞에서 배운 단어와 표현을 생각하면서 스토리를 이해해요.

Vocabulary

선잇기를 통해 배운 단어들을 확인해요.

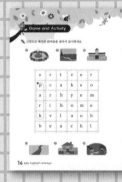

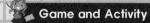

After Reading

스토리를 얼마나 이해했는지 자신의 실력을 체크해 봐요.

Game and Activity

재미있는 게임문제를 풀면서 단어를 복습해요.

차례

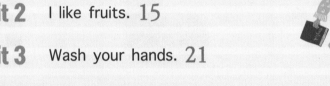

Before Reading

New Words 새 단어

park

beach

mountain

river

school

home

I

you

we

Key Expression 주요 표현

I go to the park.

① I _____ to the beach.

② I _____ to the river.

③ I _____ to school.

Story

Go to the park.

I go to the park.

I go to the beach.

You go to the mountain.

You go to the river.

We go to school.

We go home.

Vocabulary

Match the Words 낱말 연결하기

①  •

• park

②  •

• beach

③  •

• mountain

④  •

• river

⑤  •

• school

⑥  •

• home

After Reading

Write T or F 맞으면 T, 틀리면 F

①  I go to the river. _____

②  I go to the mountain. _____

③  We go to school. _____

Look and Choose 그림 보고 고르기

①  I go to the _____.

   a. park   b. river   c. mountain

②  We go _____.

   a. home   b. school   c. playground

Look and Write 그림 보고 쓰기

| we | beach | you | home | river | I |

❶ _____  go to the park.

I go to the ❷ _____ .

❸ _____  go to the mountain.

You go to the ❹ _____  .

❺ _____  go to school.

We go ❻ _____  .

Game and Activity

그림으로 제시된 단어들을 찾아서 표시하세요.

①  ②  ③

s	r	i	v	e	r
p	c	a	k	s	o
a	r	h	y	e	m
r	i	h	o	m	e
k	v	l	u	o	h
b	e	a	c	h	l

④  ⑤  ⑥

Before Reading

New Words 새 단어

apple

banana

orange

kiwi

fruit

like

Key Expression 주요 표현

I like apples.

① I _____ kiwis.

② I _____ bananas.

③ I _____ oranges.

I like fruits.

Do you like apples?

Yes, I do.

Do you like oranges?

Yes, I do.

I like kiwis and bananas, too.

I like fruits very much.

Vocabulary

Match the Words 낱말 연결하기

1.  •   • apple

2.  •   • banana

3. •   • orange

4. •   • kiwi

5. •   • like

6. •   • fruit

After Reading

Look and Choose 그림 보고 고르기

1

A: Do you like bananas?

B: Yes, I _____.

    a. do   b. does   c. did

2

I like kiwis _____ bananas, too.

    a. but   b. and   c. or

3

I like _____ very much.

    a. fish   b. food   c. fruits

Think and Choose 문장 읽고 고르기

1 This story is about _____.

    a. fruits   b. apples   c. bananas

2 Do they like fruits?

    a. yes   b. no

Look and Write 그림 보고 쓰기

| fruits   oranges   kiwis   apples   bananas |

Do you like ❶ _____ ?

Yes, I do.

Do you like ❷ _____ ?

Yes, I do.

I like ❸ _____ and ❹ _____ , too.

I like ❺ _____ very much.

✏️ 순서가 뒤섞인 알파벳을 알맞게 배열하여 쓰세요.

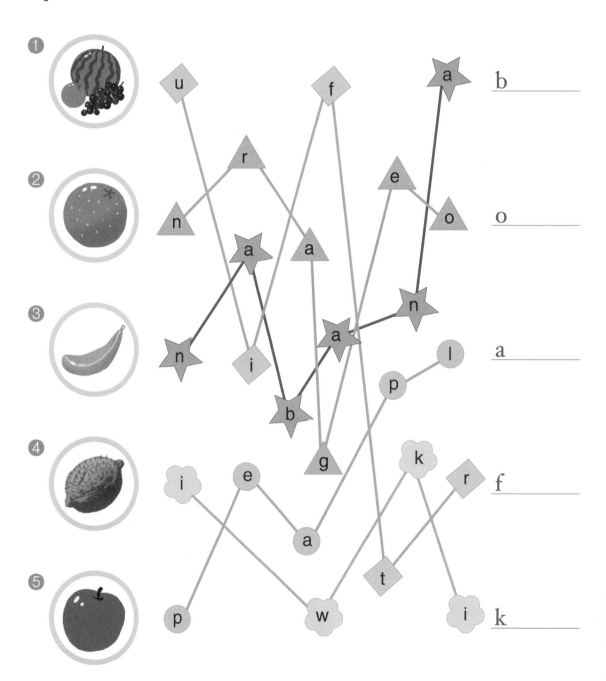

① b _____

② o _____

③ a _____

④ f _____

⑤ k _____

Before Reading

New Words 새 단어

say

wash

hands

face

hair

brush

teeth

comb

Key Expression 주요 표현

Wash your hair.

❶ _____ your face.

❷ _____ your hands.

Wash your hands.

My mom says to me.
Wash your hands.
Wash your face.
Wash your hair.
Brush your teeth.
Comb your hair.

Vocabulary

Match the Words 낱말 연결하기

①   •   • wash

②  •   • hair

③  •   • teeth

④   •   • hands

⑤   •   • brush

⑥  •   • comb

Look and Choose 그림 보고 고르기

①

_____ your hair.

a. Wash   b. Brush   c. Comb

②

Brush your _____.

a. hair   b. eyes   c. teeth

③

_____ your hair.

a. Wash   b. Comb   c. Brush

Think and Choose 문장 읽고 고르기

❶ This story is about _____.

a. eating   b. washing   c. studying

❷ Who says to the boy?

a. his mom   b. his dad   c. his teacher

Look and Write 그림 보고 쓰기

| brush | face | comb | wash | hands | hair |

My mom says to me.

① _____  your ② _____ .

Wash your ③ _____ → .

Wash your ④ _____ .

⑤ _____ your teeth.

⑥ _____  your hair.

Game and Activity

✏️ 그림을 보고 퍼즐의 빈칸을 채우세요.

①
②
③

	❶ f		❷ w		❸ b		
		❹ h					
❺ t					❻ s		

④
⑤
⑥

Before Reading

New Words 새 단어

friend

tall

short

thin

fat

lots of

Key Expression 주요 표현

Jake is tall.

❶ Jane is _____.

❷ Tony is _____.

❸ Anna is _____.

My friends

I have lots of friends.

Judy is short.

Cindy is fat.

Jake is tall.

Tom is thin.

We are good friends.

Match the Words 낱말 연결하기

①

②

③

④

⑤

⑥

• friend

• tall

• short

• thin

• fat

• lots of

After Reading

Look and Choose 그림 보고 고르기

❶

I have lots of _____.

a. friends   b. sisters   c. brothers

❷

Judy is _____.

a. tall   b. short   c. thin

❸

Tom is _____.

a. fat   b. thick   c. thin

Think and Choose 문장 읽고 고르기

❶ This story is about _____.

a. my family   b. my brothers   c. my friends

❷ Who is fat?

a. Judy   b. Cindy   c. Tom

Look and Write 그림 보고 쓰기

| short | friends | fat | tall | thin | lots of |

I have ❶ _____  friends.

Judy is ❷ _____ .

Cindy is ❸ _____ .

Jake is ❹ _____ .

Tom is ❺ _____ .

We are good ❻ _____ .

Game and Activity

🖊 사다리를 타고 내려가서 그림에 맞는 단어를 쓰세요.

❶   ❷   ❸ friend   ❹   ❺

Before Reading

New Words 새 단어

piano

violin

drum

flute

guitar

music

sister

brother

family

Key Expression 주요 표현

I play the piano.

❶ I _____ the violin.

❷ I _____ the drum.

❸ I _____ the guitar.

My family likes music.

I play the piano.

My sister plays the violin.

My brother plays the drum.

My mom plays the flute.

My dad plays the guitar.

My family likes music.

Vocabulary

Match the Words 낱말 연결하기

①  •   • piano

②  •   • violin

③  •   • drum

④  •   • flute

⑤  •   • guitar

⑥  •   • sister

Look and Choose 그림 보고 고르기

①

My sister _____ the violin.

    a. play   b. plays   c. played

②

My dad plays the _____.

    a. drum   b. guitar   c. piano

③

My _____ plays the drum.

    a. mom   b. dad   c. brother

Think and Choose 문장 읽고 고르기

❶ This story is about _____.

    a. book   b. dance   c. music

❷ Who plays the flute?

    a. mom   b. dad   c. brother

Look and Write 그림 보고 쓰기

| flute | family | sister | guitar | piano | brother |

I play the ❶ _____ .

My ❷ _____ plays the violin.

My ❸ _____ plays the drum.

My mom plays the ❹ _____ .

My dad plays the ❺ _____ .

My ❻ _____ likes music.

Game and Activity

🖊 그림에 맞는 낱말을 골라 동그라미하세요.

①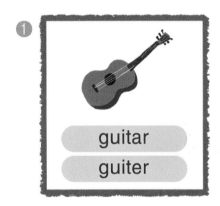

guitar

guiter

②

famili

family

③

music

musik

④

sister

sistem

⑤

brothar

brother

⑥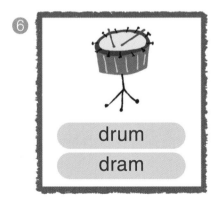

drum

dram

Before Reading

New Words 새 단어

baby

milk

boy

coke

girl

juice

man

woman

coffee

Key Expression 주요 표현

The baby drinks milk.

❶ The boy _____ coke.

❷ The girl _____ juice.

❸ The man _____ coffee.

People like to drink.

The baby drinks milk.

The boy drinks coke.

The girl drinks juice.

The man drinks coffee.

The woman drinks coffee, too.

People like to drink.

Vocabulary

Match the Words 낱말 연결하기

1   •   • milk

2  •   • boy

3   •   • juice

4   •   • coffee

5   •   • coke

6   •   • baby

After Reading

Look and Choose 그림 보고 고르기

①

The baby _____ milk.

a. drink   b. drinks   c. drinking

②

The woman drinks _____.

a. coke   b. coffee   c. water

③

People like to _____.

a. drink   b. drinks   c. drinking

Think and Choose 문장 읽고 고르기

❶ This story is about _____.

a. milk   b. watering   c. drinking

❷ Who drinks juice?

a. the girl   b. the baby   c. the woman

42 똑똑한 초등영어독해 스타터(개정판)

Look and Write 그림 보고 쓰기

| coke woman baby man juice coffee |

The ❶ _____ drinks milk.

The boy drinks ❷ _____ .

The girl drinks ❸ _____ .

The ❹ _____ drinks ❺ _____ .

The ❻ _____ drinks coffee, too.

People like to drink.

✏️ 그림으로 제시된 단어들을 찾아서 표시하세요.

①  ②  ③

j	b	o	y	c	f
m	u	c	r	o	m
b	f	i	e	f	i
a	k	w	c	f	l
b	c	o	k	e	k
y	w	r	u	e	a

④   ⑤  ⑥

Before Reading

New Words 새 단어

wear

shirt

pants

dress

sandals

what

Key Expression 주요 표현

I wear pants.

❶ I _____ a shirt.

❷ I _____ a dress.

❸ I _____ sandals.

What do you wear?

What do you wear?

I wear a shirt.

I wear pants.

What does Judy wear?

She wears a dress.

She wears sandals.

Opera House

Match the Words 낱말 연결하기

①  • • shirt

②  • • pants

③  • • dress

④ • • sandals

⑤ • • wear

⑥ • • what

Look and Choose 그림 보고 고르기

①

A: _____ do you wear?

B: I wear a shirt.

   a. Where b. Which c. What

②

A: What does Judy wear?

B: She wears a _____.

   a. shirt   b. dress   c. sandals

Think and Choose 문장 읽고 고르기

❶ This story is about _____.

   a. wearing   b. eating   c. sleeping

❷ What does Judy wear?

   a. hat   b. dress   c. shirt

Look and Write 그림 보고 쓰기

| wear shirt what dress sandals pants |

❶ _____ do you wear?

I wear a ❷ _____ .

I wear ❸ _____ .

What does Judy ❹ _____ ?

She wears a ❺ _____ .

She wears ❻ _____ .

Game and Activity

✏️ 순서가 뒤섞인 알파벳을 제대로 배열하여 쓰세요.

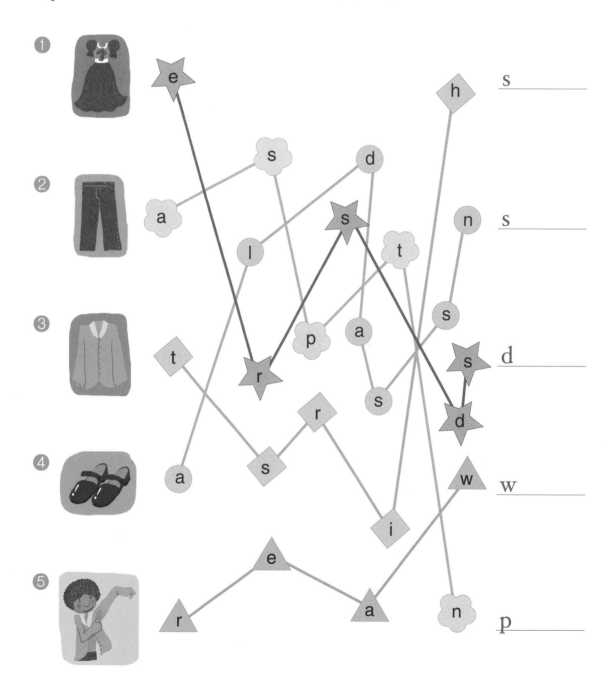

① s _____

② s _____

③ d _____

④ w _____

⑤ p _____

Before Reading

New Words 새 단어

mouth

eyes

nose

door

window

bed

open

close

touch

Key Expression 주요 표현

Open your mouth.

① _____ your eyes.

② _____ the door.

③ _____ the window.

Open and Close

Open your mouth.

Close your eyes.

Touch your nose.

Open the door.

Close the window.

Touch the bed.

Vocabulary

Match the Words 낱말 연결하기

① •   • open

② •   • close

    • touch

③ •   • eyes

④ •

    • mouth

⑤ •

⑥ •   • nose

After Reading

Write T or F 맞으면 T, 틀리면 F

① Open your eyes. _____

② Touch your nose. _____

③  Close the window. _____

Look and Choose 그림 보고 고르기

① Close your _____.

    a. eyes   b. nose   c. mouth

②  _____ the bed.

    a. Open   b. Close   c. Touch

Look and Write 그림 보고 쓰기

| window | close | nose | touch | door | open |

① _____ your mouth.

② _____ your eyes.

Touch your ③ _____ .

Open the ④ _____ .

Close the ⑤ _____ .

⑥ _____ the bed.

Game and Activity

그림을 보고 퍼즐의 빈칸을 채우세요.

①  ②  ③

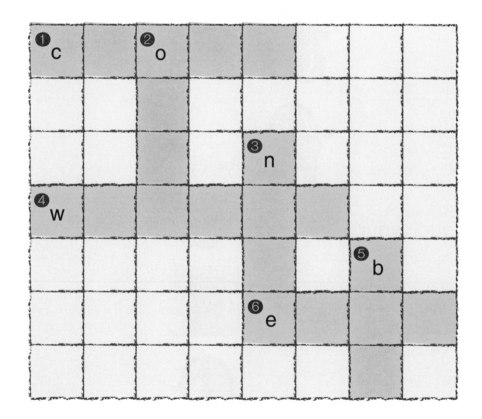

④  ⑤  ⑥

Before Reading

New Words 새 단어

desk

ruler

eraser

pencil

notebook

cat

Key Expression 주요 표현

A ruler is on the desk.

❶ An eraser is _____ the desk.

❷ A pencil is _____ the desk.

❸ A notebook is _____ the desk.

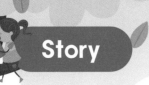

On the desk

A ruler is on my desk.

An eraser is on my desk, too.

Two notebooks are on my desk.

Three pencils are on my desk.

A cat is on my desk.

Oh, no! My notebooks!

Vocabulary

Match the Words 낱말 연결하기

①  •   • ruler

②  •   • eraser

③  •   • pencil

④  •   • cat

⑤  •   • notebook

⑥  •   • desk

Look and Choose 그림 보고 고르기

❶

A cat is on the _____.

a. bed   b. desk   c. table

❷

An _____ is on the desk.

a. ruler   b. eraser   c. pencil

❸

Two _____ are on the desk.

a. cats   b. erasers   c. notebooks

Think and Choose 문장 읽고 고르기

❶ This story is about _____.

a. my room   b. my desk   c. my pencil

❷ How many notebooks are there on the desk?

a. one   b. two   c. three

60 똑똑한 초등영어독해 스타터(개정판)

Look and Write 그림 보고 쓰기

| eraser | cat | pencils | ruler | desk | notebooks |

A ❶ _____ 　　　 is on my desk.

An ❷ _____ 　　　 is on my desk, too.

Two notebooks are on my ❸ _____ 　　　.

Three ❹ _____ 　　　 are on my desk.

A ❺ _____ 　　　 is on my desk.

Oh, no! My ❻ _____ 　　　 !

Game and Activity

✏️ 사다리를 타고 내려가서 그림에 맞는 단어를 쓰세요.

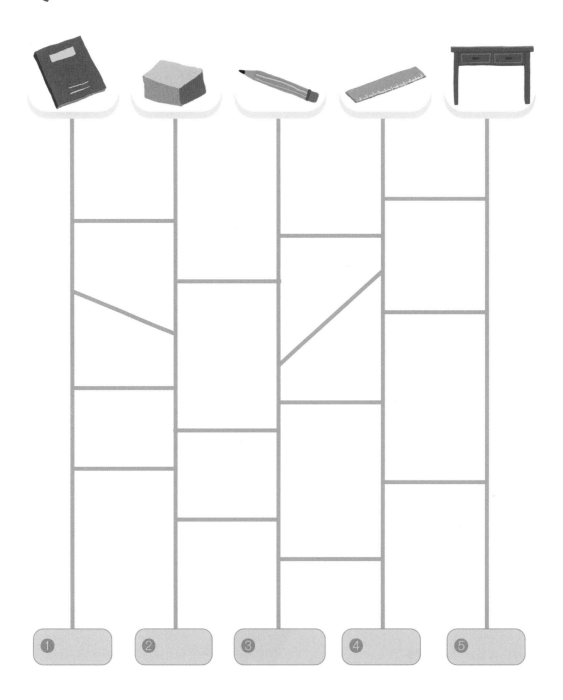

New Words 새 단어

sparrow

crow

parrot

eagle

penguin

bird

draw

Key Expression 주요 표현

I draw a sparrow.

❶ I _____ a crow.

❷ I _____ a parrot.

❸ I _____ an eagle.

Drawing birds

I draw a sparrow.

Jake draws a crow.

I draw a parrot.

Jake draws an eagle.

I draw a penguin.

We draw a lot of birds.

Vocabulary

Match the Words 낱말 연결하기

① 　　•　　•　sparrow

② 　　•　　•　crow

③ 　　•　　•　eagle

④ 　　•　　•　parrot

⑤ 　　•　　•　penguin

⑥ 　　•　　•　draw

Unit 10 **65**

After Reading

Look and Choose 그림 보고 고르기

①

Jake draws an _____.

a. crow   b. parrot   c. eagle

②

I _____ a penguin.

a. draw   b. draws   c. drew

③

We draw a lot of _____.

a. fish   b. birds   c. animals

Think and Choose 문장 읽고 고르기

❶ This story is about _____.

a. making   b. drawing   c. watching

❷ Who draws an eagle?

a. I   b. Judy   c. Jake

Look and Write 그림 보고 쓰기

| crow   eagle   draw   sparrow   penguin   parrot |

I draw a ❶ _____ .

Jake draws a ❷ _____ .

I draw a ❸ _____ .

Jake draws an ❹ _____ .

I draw a ❺ _____ .

We ❻ _____ a lot of birds.

Game and Activity

✏️ 그림에 맞는 낱말을 골라 동그라미하세요.

①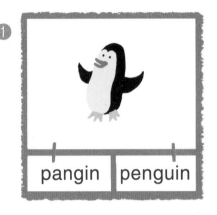

| pangin | penguin |

②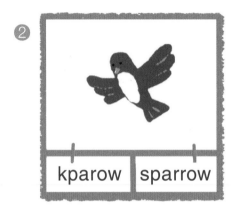

| kparow | sparrow |

③

| draw | drou |

④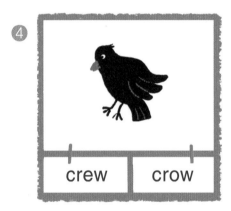

| crew | crow |

⑤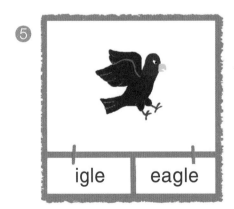

| igle | eagle |

⑥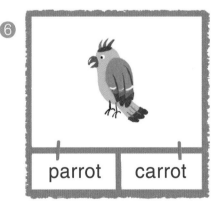

| parrot | carrot |

Before Reading

New Words 새 단어

pillow

white

blanket

purple

toy

car

robot

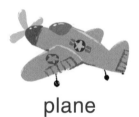

plane

Key Expression 주요 표현

My pillow is white.

❶ My car is _____.

❷ My blanket is _____.

❸ My plane is _____.

My room

Come to my room!

There is a bed.

My pillow is white.

My blanket is purple.

There are lots of toys.

I have cars, robots, and planes.

How is my room?

Vocabulary

Match the Words 낱말 연결하기

1. •   • car

2. •   • pillow

3. •   • blanket

4.  •   • white

5.  •   • purple

6.  •   • robot

After Reading

Look and Choose 그림 보고 고르기

①  Come to my _____.

a. room   b. school   c. house

②  My blanket is _____.

a. blue   b. white   c. purple

③  There are lots of _____.

a. cars   b. toys   c. planes

Think and Choose 문장 읽고 고르기

❶ This story is about _____.

a. bed   b. toys   c. room

❷ What color is his pillow?

a. white   b. purple   c. yellow

Look and Write 그림 보고 쓰기

| toys   white   pillow   planes   purple   blanket |

Come to my room!

There is a bed.

My ❶ _____ is ❷ _____ .

My ❸ _____ is ❹ _____ .

There are lots of ❺ _____  .

I have cars, robots, and ❻ _____ .

How is my room?

✏️ 그림으로 제시된 단어들을 찾아서 표시하세요.

① 　② 　③

q	p	l	a	n	e
l	i	c	a	r	w
w	l	a	s	n	h
r	l	y	t	w	i
r	o	b	o	t	t
t	w	h	y	e	e

④ 　⑤ 　⑥

Before Reading

New Words 새 단어

zoo

see

bear

lion

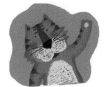
tiger

deer

monkey

animals

Key Expression 주요 표현

I see five monkeys.

❶ I _____ a bear.

❷ I _____ a tiger.

❸ I _____ a lion.

Story

Zoo

I go to the zoo.

I see one bear.

I see two lions.

I see three tigers.

I see four deers.

I see five monkeys.

There are lots of animals.

Match the Words 낱말 연결하기

①  •   • deer

② •   • monkey

③ 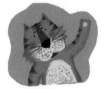 •   • lion

④ •   • tiger

⑤  •   • bear

⑥ •   • zoo

After Reading

Look and Choose 그림 보고 고르기

①  I go to the _____.

    a. zoo   b. park   c. mountain

②  I see five _____.

    a. bears   b. deers   c. monkeys

③  There are lots of _____.

    a. fish   b. birds   c. animals

Think and Choose 문장 읽고 고르기

❶ This story is about _____.

    a. bears   b. animals   c. monkeys

❷ How many tigers are there?

    a. three   b. four   c. five

Look and Write 그림 보고 쓰기

| deers   zoo   lions   animals   see   bear |

I go to the ❶ _____  .

I see one ❷ _____ .

I see two ❸ _____  .

I ❹ _____ three tigers.

I see four ❺ _____  .

I see five monkeys.

There are lots of ❻ _____ .

Game and Activity

✏️ 순서가 뒤섞인 알파벳을 제대로 배열하여 쓰세요.

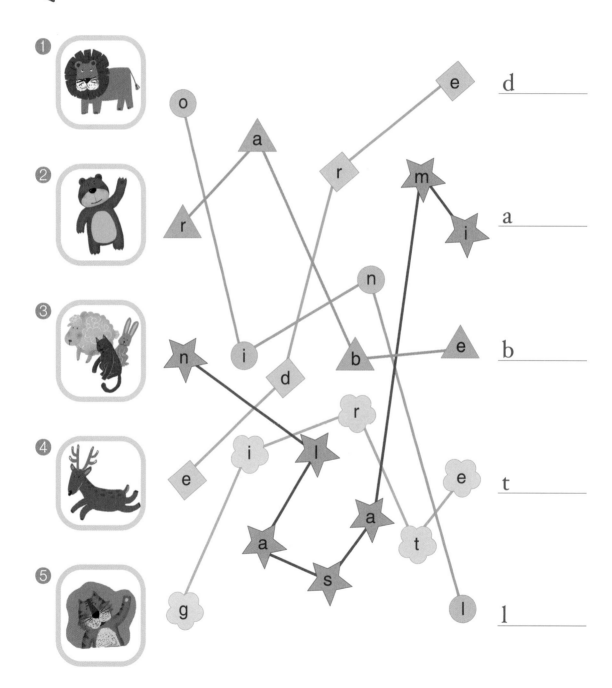

① d _____

② a _____

③ b _____

④ t _____

⑤ l _____

Before Reading

New Words 새 단어

soccer

baseball

volleyball

basketball

tennis

badminton

Key Expression 주요 표현

I play soccer.

❶ I _____ volleyball.

❷ I _____ basketball.

❸ I _____ badminton.

I play soccer.

I play soccer.

I play volleyball.

Jake plays baseball.

Jake plays basketball.

Judy plays tennis.

Judy plays badminton.

We like sports.

Vocabulary

Match the Words 낱말 연결하기

①  •   • soccer

②  •   • baseball

③  •   • volleyball

④  •   • basketball

⑤  •   • tennis

⑥  •   • badminton

Look and Choose 그림 보고 고르기

①

I _____ volleyball.

a. play   b. plays   c. played

②

Jake plays _____.

a. soccer   b. tennis   c. basketball

③

Judy plays _____.

a. tennis   b. baseball   c. badminton

Think and Choose 문장 읽고 고르기

❶ This story is about _____.

a. sports   b. dream   c. soccer

❷ What sport does Jake play?

a. soccer   b. baseball   c. volleyball

Look and Write 그림 보고 쓰기

| basketball   tennis   baseball   soccer   badminton   volleyball |

I play ❶ _____ .

I play ❷ _____ .

Jake plays ❸ _____ .

Jake plays ❹ _____ .

Judy plays ❺ _____ .

Judy plays ❻ _____ .

We like sports.

Game and Activity

그림을 보고 퍼즐의 빈칸을 채우세요.

①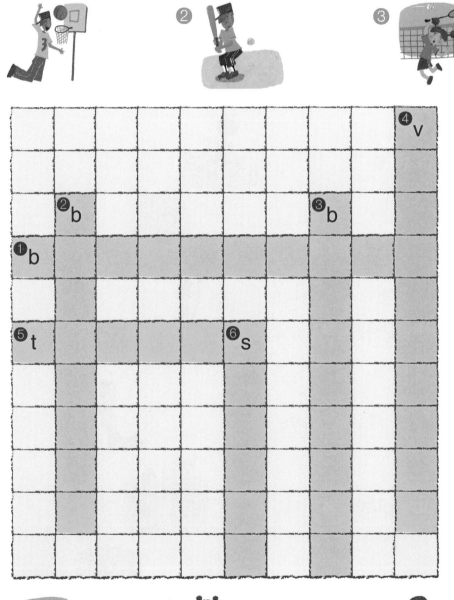

②

③

④ v

②b

③b

①b

⑤t

⑥s

④

⑤

⑥

Before Reading

New Words 새 단어

mouse

cake

mice

on

under

behind

in front of

around

next to

Key Expression 주요 표현

One mouse is
on the cake.

❶ One mouse is _____ the cake.

❷ One mouse is _____ the desk.

❸ One mouse is _____ the chair.

There are five mice.

One mouse is on the cake.

One mouse is under the cake.

One mouse is behind the cake.

One mouse is in front of the cake.

One mouse is next to the cake.

There are five mice around the cake.

Match the Words 낱말 연결하기

1   •   • on

2   •   • under

3   •   • behind

4   •   • next to

5   •   • in front of

6      •   • around

After Reading

Look and Choose 그림 보고 고르기

1 One _____ is on the cake.

a. lion   b. mouse   c. monkey

2 One mouse is _____ to the cake.

a. next   b. under   c. behind

3 There are five _____ around the cake.

a. mouse   b. mice   c. mouses

Think and Choose 문장 읽고 고르기

❶ This story is about _____.

a. bed   b. mice   c. food

❷ How many mice are there?

a. five   b. six   c. seven

Look and Write 그림 보고 쓰기

| mouse | next to | behind | on | cake | mice |

One mouse is ❶ _____ the cake.

One mouse is under the ❷ _____ .

One mouse is ❸ _____ the cake.

One ❹ _____ is in front of the cake.

One mouse is ❺ _____ the cake.

There are five ❻ _____ around the cake.

✏️ 사다리를 타고 내려가서 그림에 맞는 단어를 쓰세요.

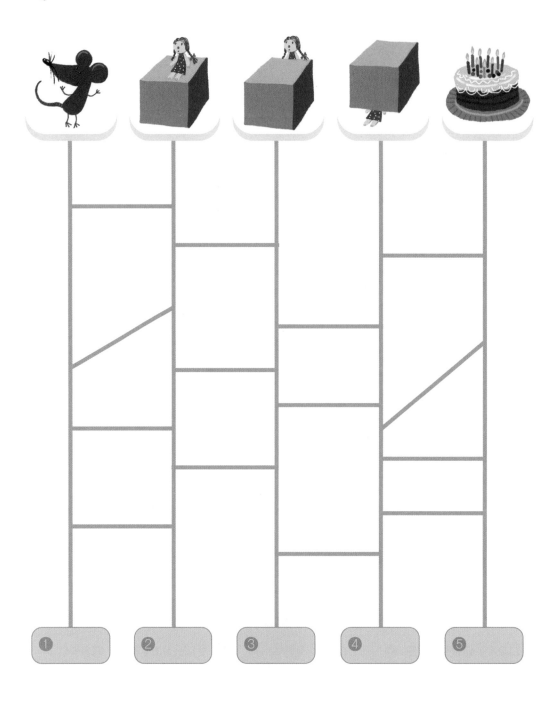

Before Reading

New Words 새 단어

Monday

Tuesday

Wednesday

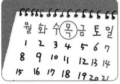

Thursday

Friday

Saturday

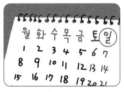

Sunday

peach

strawberry

Key Expression 주요 표현

We eat oranges
on Friday.

❶ We eat apples ____ _____.

❷ We eat peaches ____ _____.

❸ We eat bananas ____ _____.

We eat fruits.

We eat apples on Monday.

We eat bananas on Tuesday.

We eat kiwis on Wednesday.

We eat peaches on Thursday.

We eat oranges on Friday.

We eat strawberries on Saturday.

We have nothing on Sunday.

Vocabulary

Match the Words 낱말 연결하기

  •   • Monday

  •   • Tuesday

  •   • Wednesday

  •   • Thursday

  •   • Friday

  •   • Saturday

Look and Choose 그림 보고 고르기

① We _____ bananas on Tuesday.

    a. buy   b. take   c. eat

② We eat peaches on _____.

    a. Sunday   b. Tuesday   c. Thursday

③ We eat _____ on Saturday.

    a. kiwis   b. apples   c. strawberries

Think and Choose 문장 읽고 고르기

❶ This story is about _____.

    a. drinking   b. eating   c. making

❷ When do they eat kiwis?

    a. Tuesday   b. Thursday   c. Wednesday

Look and Write 그림 보고 쓰기

> Tuesday   Monday   peaches
> Friday   strawberries   Wednesday

We eat apples on ❶ _____  .

We eat bananas on ❷ _____  .

We eat kiwis on ❸ _____ .

We eat ❹ _____ on Thursday.

We eat oranges on ❺ _____ .

We eat ❻ _____ on Saturday.

We have nothing on Sunday.

Game and Activity

그림을 보고 알맞은 낱말을 골라 동그라미하세요.

①
Friday

Sunday

②
orange

strawberry

③
Thursday

Monday

④
Wednesday

Saturday

⑤
peach

Kiwi

⑥
Tuesday

Nothing

Before Reading

New Words 새 단어

weather

sunny

warm

ride

bicycle

walk

Key Expression 주요 표현

A: How is the weather?
B: It's sunny.

A: How is the _____ today?

B: It's warm.

Weather

How is the weather today?

It's sunny and warm.

Wow, great!

Let's ride a bicycle!

Let's take a walk!

Let's play baseball!

Match the Words 낱말 연결하기

① •   • sunny

②  •   • weather

③  •   • warm

④ •   • walk

⑤  •   • bicycle

⑥ •   • ride

After Reading

Look and Choose 그림 보고 고르기

1.

   A: How is the weather?
   B: It's _____.
   a. rainy   b. sunny   c. windy

2.

   Let's _____ a bicycle.
   a. ride   b. close   c. wash

3.

   Let's take a _____.
   a. walks   b. walk   c. walked

Think and Choose 문장 읽고 고르기

1. How is the weather today?

   a. cool   b. warm   c. cold

2. What will they ride?

   a. bus   b. car   c. bicycle

Look and Write 그림 보고 쓰기

| warm | walk | weather | sunny | bicycle | ride |

How is the ❶ _____ today?

It's ❷ _____ and ❸ _____ .

Wow, great!

Let's ❹ _____ a ❺ _____ !

Let's take a ❻ _____  !

Let's play baseball!

Game and Activity

✏️ 그림으로 제시된 단어들을 찾아서 표시하세요.

a	w	v	x	w	a	r	m
h	z	e	j	o	t	d	p
z	i	w	a	l	k	o	u
c	a	g	b	t	z	y	m
d	r	x	s	u	h	w	q
b	i	c	y	c	l	e	v
g	d	d	k	n	b	h	r
t	e	w	s	u	n	n	y

Before Reading

New Words 새 단어

baby

elephant

giraffe

panda

all

cute

Key Expression 주요 표현

A: Who am I?
B: You are an
   elephant's baby.

A: _____ am I?

B: You are a giraffe's baby.

Who am I?

Who am I?

You are an elephant's baby.

Who am I?

You are a giraffe's baby.

Who am I?

You are a panda's baby.

You are all cute babies.

Vocabulary

Match the Words 낱말 연결하기

①  •

• panda

② 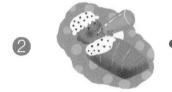 •

• giraffe

③  •

• baby

④  •

• elephant

⑤  •

• all

After Reading

Look and Choose 그림 보고 고르기

①

A: Who am I?

B: You are a _____ baby.

  a. bear's   b. tiger's   c. panda's

②

A: _____ am I?

B: You are a giraffe's baby.

  a. How   b. Who   c. What

Think and Choose 문장 읽고 고르기

① This story is about _____.

  a. boy   b. daughter   c. baby

② Babies are very _____.

  a. cute   b. strange   c. large

Look and Write 그림 보고 쓰기

| panda's   elephant's   cute   all   giraffe's |

Who am I?

You are an ❶ _____ baby.

Who am I?

You are a ❷ _____ baby.

Who am I?

You are a ❸ _____ baby.

You are ❹ _____ ❺ _____ babies.

Game and Activity

순서가 뒤섞인 알파벳을 제대로 배열하여 쓰세요.

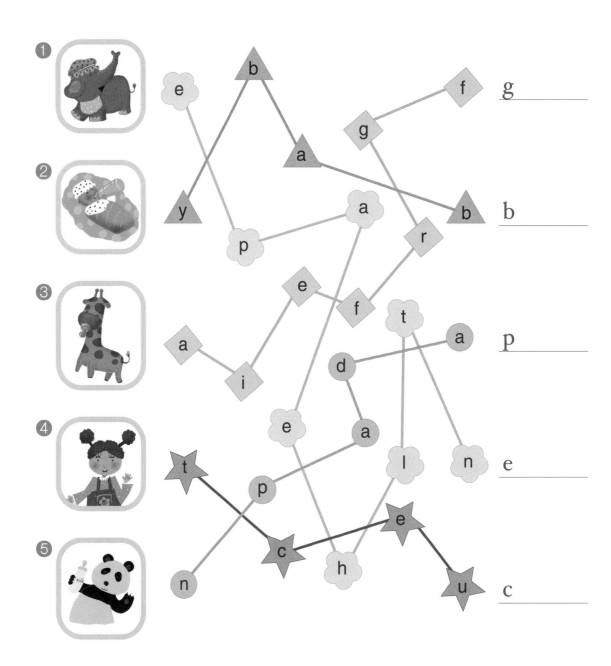

① g _____

② b _____

③ p _____

④ e _____

⑤ c _____

Before Reading

New Words 새 단어

grass

tulip

rose

lily

butterfly

dragonfly

beautiful

garden

Key Expression 주요 표현

I draw green grass.

❶ I draw _____ leaves.

❷ I draw a _____ mountain.

❸ I draw a _____ caterpillar.

What a beautiful garden!

I draw green grass.

I draw blue tulips.

I draw red roses.

I draw white lilies.

I draw yellow butterflies.

I draw purple dragonflies.

What a beautiful garden!

Vocabulary

Match the Words 낱말 연결하기

 ①  •   • dragonfly

 ② •   • grass

 ③  •   • rose

 ④  •   • lily

⑤ •   • butterfly

⑥  •   • garden

Look and Choose 그림 보고 고르기

1

I draw _____ tulips.

a. white   b. blue   c. yellow

2

I draw purple _____.

a. tulips   b. lilies   c. dragonflies

3

What a beautiful _____!

a. park   b. ground   c. garden

Think and Choose 문장 읽고 고르기

1 This story is about _____.

a. watching   b. drawing   c. making

2 What color is the grass?

a. yellow   b. green   c. white

Look and Write 그림 보고 쓰기

| lilies   grass   garden   roses   dragonflies   tulips |

I draw green ❶ _____ .

I draw blue ❷ _____ .

I draw red ❸ _____ .

I draw white ❹ _____ .

I draw yellow butterflies.

I draw purple ❺ _____ .

What a beautiful ❻ _____ !

Game and Activity

✏️ 그림을 보고 빈 칸 채우기

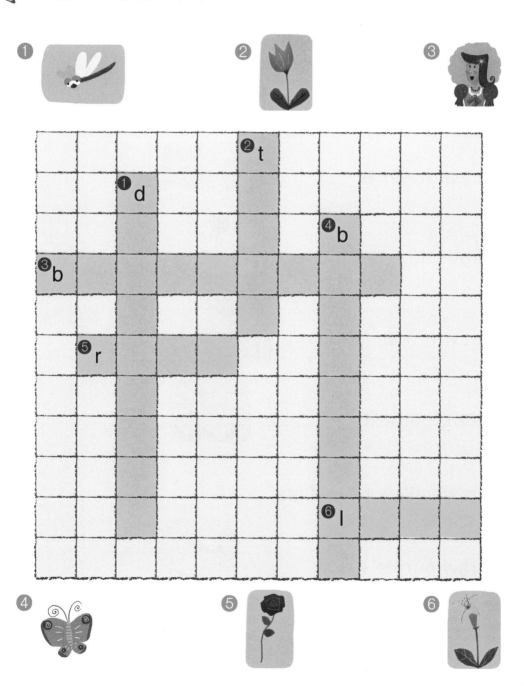

① ❷t
❶d
❹b
❸b
❺r
❻l

New Words 새 단어

pig

cow

horse

hen

dog

lamb

Key Expression 주요 표현

A pig says oink oink.

① A horse _____ neigh neigh.

② A hen _____ cock-a-doodle.

③ A lamb _____ baa baa.

An animals' Song

A pig says oink oink.

A cow says moo moo.

A horse says neigh neigh.

A hen says cock-a-doodle.

A dog says woof woof.

A lamb says baa baa.

This is an animals' song.

Match the Words 낱말 연결하기

1.  •

• lamb

2.  •

• hen

3.  •

• cow

4.  •

• pig

5.  •

• dog

6.  •

• horse

After Reading

Look and Choose 그림 보고 고르기

1

A lamb says _____.

a. baa baa　b. neigh neigh　c. oink oink

2

A _____ says cock-a-doodle.

a. hen　　b. cow　　c. horse

3

A dog _____ woof woof.

a. says　　b. sings　　c. dances

Think and Choose 문장 읽고 고르기

1 This story is about animals' _____.

a. playing　　b. sleeping　　c. saying

2 How many animals are there?

a. five　　b. six　　c. seven

Look and Write 그림 보고 쓰기

| pig | hen | horse | dog | lamb | cow |

A ❶ _____ says oink oink.

A ❷ _____ says moo moo.

A ❸ _____ says neigh neigh.

A ❹ _____ says cock-a-doodle.

A ❺ _____ says woof woof.

A ❻ _____ says baa baa.

This is an animals' song.

Game and Activity

✏️ 사다리를 타고 내려가서 그림에 맞는 단어를 쓰세요.

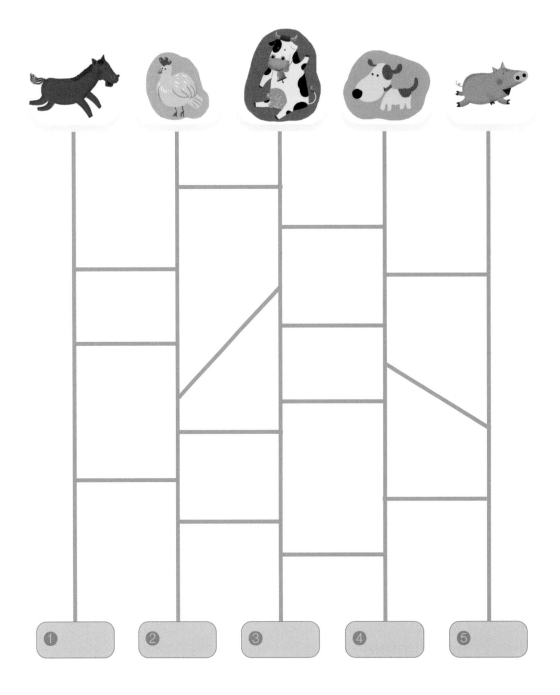

① ② ③ ④ ⑤

Before Reading

New Words 새 단어

sky

two

wing

tree

squirrel

four

leg

ground

snake

Key Expression 주요 표현

Look at the sky.

1 _____ at the tree.

2 _____ at the bird.

3 _____ at the ground.

Poor snake!

Look at the sky!

A bird has two wings.

Look at the tree!

A squirrel has four legs.

Look at the ground!

A snake has no wings and no legs.

Oh, poor snake!

Vocabulary

Match the Words 낱말 연결하기

1.  •   • sky

2.  •   • wing

3.  •   • ground

4.  •   • snake

5. •   • squirrel

6.  •   • leg

After Reading

Write T or F 맞으면 T, 틀리면 F

①
A bird has three wings. _____

②
Look at the ground! _____

③
A snake has no wings and no legs.

_____

Look and Choose 그림 보고 고르기

①
_____ at the sky.

a. See   b. Look   c. Watch

②
A squirrel has four _____.

a. wings   b. hands   c. legs

Look and Write 그림 보고 쓰기

| two   snake   sky   ground   tree   squirrel |

Look at the ❶ _____ !

A bird has ❷ _____ wings.

Look at the ❸ _____ !

A ❹ _____ has four legs.

Look at the ❺ _____  !

A ❻ _____  has no wings and no legs.

Oh, poor snake!

그림을 보고 알맞은 낱말을 골라 동그라미하세요.

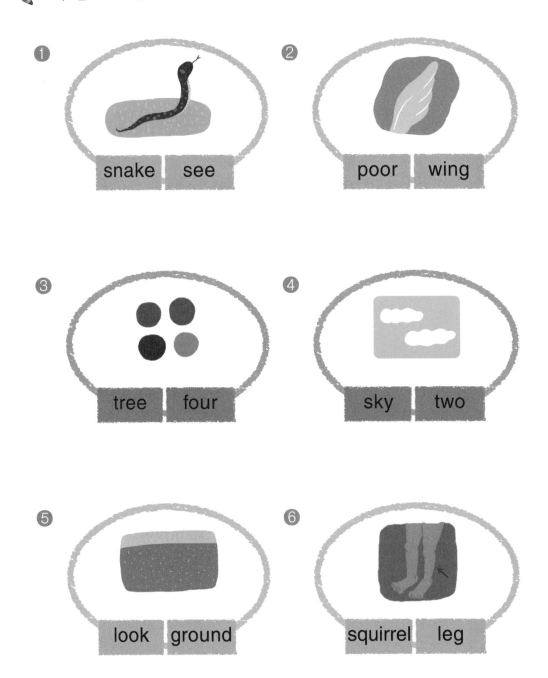

① snake see

② poor wing

③ tree four

④ sky two

⑤ look ground

⑥ squirrel leg

스토리 해석 및 정답

Unit 1

 Before Reading   9p

Key Expression

① ② ③ go

 Story   10p

공원에 가요.

나는 공원에 가요.
나는 해변에 가요.
너는 산에 가요.
너는 강에 가요.
우리는 학교에 가요.
우리는 집에 가요.

 Vocabulary   11p

Match the Words

① home   ② river
③ mountain   ④ park
⑤ beach   ⑥ school

 After Reading   12~13p

Write T or F

① F   ② F   ③ T

Look and Choose

① a   ② a

Look and Write

① I   ② beach   ③ You
④ river   ⑤ We   ⑥ home

 **Game and Activity**   14p

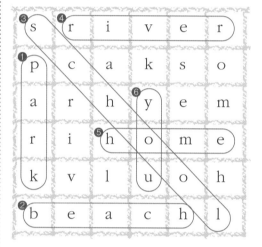

Unit 2

 Before Reading   15p

Key Expression

① ② ③ like

 Story   16p

나는 과일을 좋아해.

너는 사과를 좋아하니?
응, 좋아해.

너는 오렌지를 좋아하니?
응, 좋아해.
나는 키위와 바나나도 좋아해.
나는 과일을 아주 좋아해.

Vocabulary   17p

Match the Words

① fruit   ② like   ③ apple

④ banana   ⑤ kiwi   ⑥ orange

After Reading   18~19p

Look and Choose

① a   ② b   ③ c

Think and Choose

① a   ② a

Look and Write

① apples   ② oranges

③ kiwis   ④ bananas

⑤ fruits

Game and Activity   20p

① fruit   ② orange

③ banana   ④ kiwi

⑤ apple

Unit 3

Before Reading   21p

Key Expression

① ② Wash

Story   22p

손을 씻어라.

엄마가 나에게 말해요.
손을 씻어라.
얼굴을 씻어라.
머리를 감아라.
이를 닦아라.
머리를 빗어라.

Vocabulary   23p

Match the Words

① hair   ② wash   ③ hands

④ teeth   ⑤ comb   ⑥ brush

After Reading   24~25p

Look and Choose

① a   ② c   ③ b

Think and Choose

① b   ② a

Look and Write

① Wash ② hands ③ face
④ hair ⑤ Brush ⑥ Comb

Game and Activity   26p

① face ② wash ③ brush
④ hair ⑤ teeth ⑥ say

Unit 4

Before Reading   27p

Key Expression

① ② ③ tall

Story   28p

나의 친구들

나는 친구들이 많아요.
주디는 키가 작아요.
신디는 뚱뚱해요.
제이크는 키가 커요.
탐은 말랐어요.
우리는 좋은 친구들이에요.

Vocabulary   29p

Match the Words

① thin ② tall ③ lots of

---

④ short ⑤ fat ⑥ friend

After Reading   30~31p

Look and Choose

① a ② b ③ c

Think and Choose

① c ② b

Look and Write

① lots of ② short ③ fat
④ tall ⑤ thin ⑥ friends

Game and Activity   32p

① fat ② tall ③ friend
④ short ⑤ thin

Unit 5

Before Reading   33p

Key Expression

① ② ③ play

Story   34p

우리 가족은 음악을 좋아해요.

나는 피아노를 연주해요.
언니는 바이올린을 연주해요.

오빠는 드럼을 쳐요.
엄마는 플루트를 불어요.
아빠는 기타를 쳐요.
우리 가족은 음악을 좋아해요.

Vocabulary 35p

Match the Words

① drum ② flute ③ piano
④ violin ⑤ sister ⑥ guitar

After Reading 36~37p

Look and Choose

① b ② b ③ c

Think and Choose

① c ② a

Look and Write

① piano ② sister
③ brother ④ flute
⑤ guitar ⑥ family

Game and Activity 38p

① guitar ② family
③ music ④ sister
⑤ brother ⑥ drum

Unit 6

Before Reading 39p

Key Expression

① ② ③ drinks

Story 40p

사람들은 마시는 것을 좋아해요.

아기가 우유를 마셔요.
소년은 콜라를 마셔요.
소녀는 주스를 마셔요.
남자는 커피를 마셔요.
여자도 커피를 마셔요.
사람들은 마시는 것을 좋아해요.

Vocabulary 41p

Match the Words

① coffee ② baby ③ milk
④ coke ⑤ boy ⑥ juice

After Reading 42~43p

Look and Choose

① b ② b ③ a

Think and Choose

① c ② a

Look and Write

① baby ② coke ③ juice

④ man ⑤ coffee ⑥ woman

 Game and Activity 44p

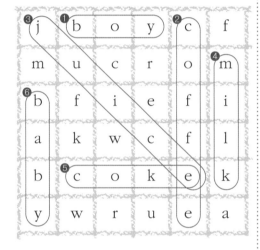

나는 바지를 입어.
주디는 뭘 입니?
그녀는 드레스를 입어.
그녀는 샌들을 신어.

 Vocabulary 47p

Match the Words

① dress ② what ③ pants

④ wear ⑤ sandals ⑥ shirt

After Reading 48~49p

Look and Choose

① c ② b

Think and Choose

① a ② b

Look and Write

① What ② shirt

③ pants ④ wear

⑤ dress ⑥ sandals

Key Expression

① ② ③ wear

Story 46p

너는 뭘 입니?

너는 뭘 입니?
나는 셔츠를 입어.

Game and Activity 50p

① dress ② pants

③ shirt ④ sandals

⑤ wear

Game and Activity   68p

1. penguin   2. sparrow
3. draw   4. crow
5. eagle   6. parrot

Unit 11

Before Reading   69p

Key Expression
1. 2. 3. white

Story   70p

나의 방

나의 방으로 오세요.
침대가 하나 있어요.
나의 베개는 흰색이에요.
나의 이불은 보라색이에요.
장난감들이 많이 있어요.
나는 자동차, 로봇, 그리고 비행기가
있어요.
나의 방은 어때요?

Vocabulary   71p

Match the Words
1. robot   2. purple

3. white   4. blanket
5. pillow   6. car

After Reading   72~73p

Look and Choose
1. a   2. c   3. b

Think and Choose
1. c   2. a

Look and Write
1. pillow   2. white
3. blanket   4. purple
5. toys   6. planes

Game and Activity   74p

q	⑥p	l	a	n	e
①l	i	②c	a	r	④w
w	l	a	s	n	h
r	l	y	⑤t	w	i
③r	o	b	o	t	t
t	w	h	y	e	e

Unit 12

Before Reading
75p

Key Expression

1 2 3 see

Story
76p

동물원

나는 동물원에 가요.
나는 곰 한 마리를 봐요.
나는 사자 두 마리를 봐요.
나는 호랑이 세 마리를 봐요.
나는 사슴 네 마리를 봐요.
나는 원숭이 다섯 마리를 봐요.
동물들이 많이 있어요.

Vocabulary
77p

Match the Words

1 bear **2** zoo **3** deer
4 tiger **5** monkey **6** lion

After Reading
78~79p

Look and Choose

1 a **2** c **3** c

Think and Choose

1 b **2** a

Look and Write

1 zoo **2** bear **3** lions
4 see **5** deers **6** animals

Game and Activity
80p

1 lion **2** bear **3** animals
4 deer **5** tiger

Unit 13

Before Reading
81p

Key Expression

1 2 3 play

Story
82p

나는 축구를 해요.

나는 축구를 해요.
나는 배구를 해요.
제이크는 야구를 해요.
제이크는 농구를 해요.
주디는 테니스를 쳐요.
주디는 배드민턴을 쳐요.
우리는 스포츠를 좋아해요.

Vocabulary 83p

Match the Words

① basketball ② tennis

③ soccer ④ badminton

⑤ baseball ⑥ volleyball

After Reading 84~85p

Look and Choose

① a ② c ③ c

Think and Choose

① a ② b

Look and Write

① soccer ② volleyball

③ baseball ④ basketball

⑤ tennis ⑥ badminton

Game and Activity 86p

① basketball ② baseball

③ badminton ④ volleyball

⑤ tennis ⑥ soccer

Unit 14

Before Reading 87p

Key Expression

① ② ③ on

Story 88p

쥐 다섯 마리가 있어요.

쥐 한 마리가 케이크 위에 있어요.
쥐 한 마리가 케이크 아래에 있어요.
쥐 한 마리가 케이크 뒤에 있어요.
쥐 한 마리가 케이크 앞에 있어요.
쥐 한 마리가 케이크 바로 옆에 있어요.
쥐 다섯 마리가 케이크 주변에 있어요.

Vocabulary 89p

Match the Words

① next to ② on

③ in front of ④ under

⑤ behind ⑥ around

After Reading 90~91p

Look and Choose

① b ② a ③ b

Think and Choose

① b ② a

Look and Write

① on   ② cake   ③ behind

④ mouse   ⑤ next to   ⑥ mice

Game and Activity   92p

① mouse   ② cake   ③ under

④ behind   ⑤ on

Unit 15

Before Reading   93p

Key Expression

① ② ③ on Friday

Story   94p

우리는 과일을 먹어요.

우리는 월요일에 사과를 먹어요.
우리는 화요일에 바나나를 먹어요.
우리는 수요일에 키위를 먹어요.
우리는 목요일에 복숭아를 먹어요.
우리는 금요일에 오렌지를 먹어요.
우리는 토요일에 딸기를 먹어요.
우리는 일요일에 아무것도 없어요.

Vocabulary   95p

Match the Words

① Tuesday   ② Monday

③ Saturday   ④ Friday

⑤ Wednesday   ⑥ Thursday

After Reading   96~97p

Look and Choose

① c   ② c   ③ c

Think and Choose

① b   ② c

Look and Write

① Monday   ② Tuesday

③ Wednesday   ④ peaches

⑤ Friday   ⑥ strawberries

Game and Activity   98p

① Friday   ② strawberry

③ Monday   ④ Saturday

⑤ peach   ⑥ Tuesday

Unit 16

 Before Reading   99p

Key Expression

weather

Story   100p

날씨

오늘 날씨가 어때?
화창하고 따뜻해.
우와, 잘 됐다.
자전거 타자!
산책하자!
야구하자!

 Vocabulary   101p

Match the Words

① ride   ② sunny   ③ weather
④ bicycle   ⑤ warm   ⑥ walk

After Reading   102~103p

Look and Choose

① b   ② a   ③ b

Think and Choose

① b   ② c

Look and Write

① weather   ② sunny
③ warm   ④ ride
⑤ bicycle   ⑥ walk

 Game and Activity   104p

a	①w	v	x	⑤w	a	r	m
h	z	e	j	o	t	d	p
z	i	②w	a	l	k	o	u
c	a	g	b	t	z	y	m
d	⑥r	x	s	u	h	w	q
③b	i	c	y	c	l	e	v
g	d	d	k	n	b	h	r
t	e	w	④s	u	n	n	y

Unit 17

 Before Reading   105p

Key Expression

Who

After Reading 114~115p

Look and Choose
❶ b   ❷ c   ❸ c

Think and Choose
❶ b   ❷ b

Look and Write
❶ grass   ❷ tulips
❸ roses   ❹ lilies
❺ dragonflies   ❻ garden

Game and Activity 116p

❶ dragonfly   ❷ tulip
❸ beautiful   ❹ butterfly
❺ rose   ❻ lily

Unit 19

Before Reading 117p

Key Expression
❶ ❷ ❸ says

Story 118p

동물들의 노래
돼지는 꿀꿀 소리를 내요.
소는 음메 음메 소리를 내요.
말은 히잉 히잉 소리를 내요.
암탉은 꼬끼오 소리를 내요.
강아지는 멍멍 소리를 내요.
양은 매에 매에 소리를 내요.
이것은 동물들의 노래예요.

Vocabulary 119p

Match the Words
❶ dog   ❷ pig   ❸ horse
❹ cow   ❺ lamb   ❻ hen

After Reading 120~121p

Look and Choose
❶ a   ❷ a   ❸ a

Think and Choose
❶ c   ❷ b

Look and Write
❶ pig   ❷ cow   ❸ horse
❹ hen   ❺ dog   ❻ lamb

> **불쌍한 뱀!**
>
> 하늘을 봐요!
> 새는 날개가 두 개 있어요.
> 나무를 봐요!
> 다람쥐는 다리가 네 개 있어요.
> 땅을 봐요!
> 뱀은 날개도 없고, 다리도 없어요.
> 오, 불쌍한 뱀!